Super Simple
Hop & Jump

Healthy & Fun Activities to Move Your Body

Nancy Tuminelly

Contributing Physical Education Consultant, Linn Ahrendt, Power Play Education, Inc.
Consulting Editor, Diane Craig, M.A./Reading Specialist

A Division of ABDO

ABDO
Publishing Company

visit us at www.abdopublishing.com

Published by ABDO Publishing Company, a division of the ABDO Group, P.O. Box 398166, Minneapolis, Minnesota 55439. Copyright © 2012 by Abdo Consulting Group, Inc. International copyrights reserved in all countries. No part of this book may be reproduced in any form without written permission from the publisher. Super SandCastle™ is a trademark and logo of ABDO Publishing Company.

Printed in the United States of America, North Mankato, Minnesota

052011
092011

 PRINTED ON RECYCLED PAPER

Editor: Liz Salzmann
Content Development: Nancy Tuminelly, Linn Ahrendt
Cover and Interior Design and Production: Colleen Dolphin, Mighty Media, Inc.
Photo Credits: Colleen Dolphin, Shutterstock

Library of Congress Cataloging-in-Publication Data

Tuminelly, Nancy, 1952-
  Super simple hop & jump : healthy & fun activities to move your body / Nancy Tuminelly.
    p. cm. -- (Super simple exercise)
  ISBN 978-1-61714-960-3
  1. Physical fitness for children--Juvenile literature. 2. Jumping--Juvenile literature. I. Title.
  GV443.T855 2012
  613.7'042--dc22
                                                                                    2011000979

Super SandCastle™ books are created by a team of professional educators, reading specialists, and content developers around five essential components—phonemic awareness, phonics, vocabulary, text comprehension, and fluency—to assist young readers as they develop reading skills and strategies and increase their general knowledge. All books are written, reviewed, and leveled for guided reading, early reading intervention, and Accelerated Reader® programs for use in shared, guided, and independent reading and writing activities to support a balanced approach to literacy instruction.

Note to Adults

This book is all about encouraging children to be active and play! Avoid having children compete against each other. At this age, the idea is for them to have fun and learn basic skills. Some of the activities in the book require adult assistance and/or permission. Make sure children play in appropriate spaces free of objects that can cause accidents or injuries. Stay with children at the park, playground, or mall, or when going for a walk. Make sure children wear appropriate shoes and clothing for comfort and ease of movement.

Contents

Time to Hop & Jump!

Being active is one part of being healthy. You should move your body for at least one hour every day! You don't have to do it all at one time. It all adds up.

Being active gives you **energy** and helps your body grow strong. There are super simple ways to move your body. Two of them are hopping and jumping. This book has fun and easy activities to get you started. Try them or make up your own.

Do You Know?
Being Active Helps You

1 be more relaxed and less stressed

2 feel better about yourself and what you can do

3 be more ready to learn and do well in school

4 rest better and sleep well at night

5 build strong bones, **muscles**, and joints

So turn off the TV, computer, or phone. Get up and start bending and stretching!

Muscle Mania

You have **muscles** all over your body. You use them whenever you move any part of your body. The more you move your muscles, the stronger they get!

shoulder

arm

neck

stomach

chest

back

upper leg

lower leg

Healthy Eating

You need **energy** to move your body. Good food gives your body energy. Some good foods are fruits, vegetables, milk, lean meat, fish, and bread. Foods such as pizza, hamburgers, French fries, and candy are okay sometimes. But you shouldn't eat them all the time.

 ## Remember!

- Eating right every day is as important as being active every day

- Eat three healthy meals every day

- Eat five **servings** of fruits and vegetables every day

- Eat healthy snacks

- Eat fewer fast foods

- Drink a lot of water

- Eat less sugar, salt, and fat

Move It Chart

Make a chart to record how much time you spend doing things. Put your chart where you will see it often. This will help you remember to fill it out every day. See if you move your body at least an hour each day.

Move It Chart
Week of March 8-14

Activity	Sunday	Monday	Tuesday	Wednesday	Thursday	Friday	Saturday
soccer	●		●	●	●		●
Leaping Lizards		●				●	
mow the lawn			●				

1 Put the title of your chart at the top of a piece of paper. Then put "Week of" and a line for the dates.

2 Make a chart with eight **columns**. Put "activity" at the top of the first column. Put the days of the week at the top of the other columns. Under "activity," list all of the things you do. Include sports, games, and **chores**. Don't forget the activities in this book! Put "total time" at the bottom. Make copies of the chart.

3 Start a new chart each week. Put the dates at the top.

4 Mark how much time you spend on each activity each day. Be creative! Use different colors, **symbols**, or clock faces. For example, a blue sticker could mean 15 minutes of movement. A purple sticker could mean 60 minutes of movement.

⬤ = 10 minutes ⬤ = 30 minutes
⬤ = 15 minutes ⬤ = 60 minutes

5 Add up each day's activity. Did you move your body at least an hour every day?

Tools & Supplies

Here are some of the things you will need to get started.

zipper bags

dried beans

masking tape

rope

tape measure

small rock

bubble wrap

markers

athletic shoe

duct tape

jump rope

chalk

large paper plates

rubber bands

yardstick

Get Over It

Books aren't just for reading anymore!

WHAT YOU NEED

10 books
tape measure
paper
markers

MUSCLES USED

leg

TIME

5-10 minutes

1. Put the books on the floor in a line about 12 inches (30 cm) apart.

2. Make START and FINISH signs. Put one at each end of the line of books.

3. Start in front of the first book. Jump over it with both feet. Then jump over the next book.

4. Keep jumping over the books until you reach the end. Go as fast as you can. Try not to stop between jumps.

➡ When playing with others, see who is the fastest. Use a stopwatch to time each jumper. This will get everyone moving and breathing fast!

Rubber Band Rope

A stretchy jump rope for loads of jumping fun!

WHAT YOU NEED

box of rubber bands
tape measure

MUSCLES USED

leg
arm
back

TIME

10–15 minutes

1. Tie rubber bands together to make a rubber band rope. It should be about 10 feet (3 m) long. Tie the ends together.

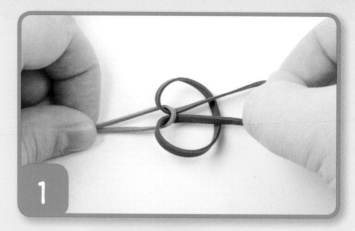

2. Have two people stand about 5 feet (1.5 m) apart. They should wrap the rubber band rope around their **ankles**.

3. Another person jumps so both feet land inside the rope.

4. Then the jumper jumps so both feet land outside the rope.

5. Next the jumper jumps so both feet land on the rope.

6. Do the jumps again. Try to do them faster. If the jumper messes up, it's someone else's turn.

Toy Hurdle Course

Use your toys as objects to jump over!

WHAT YOU NEED

10 toys, different sizes
paper
markers
masking tape

MUSCLES USED

leg
arm
back

TIME

10-15 minutes

1. Spread the toys out on the floor. Make 10 small signs. Number them from 1 to 10. Tape a number to each toy. This is the order you will jump over the toys.

2. Make START and FINISH signs with paper and markers. Put them where you will begin and end the course.

3. Begin at the start. Hop on one foot to the first toy. Jump over the toy with both feet.

4. **Switch** feet and hop to the next toy. Jump over it. Continue until you reach the finish.

✋ Do not use balls or anything that rolls! So no skateboards or toy cars or trucks!

Leaping Lizards

How far can you jump?

WHAT YOU NEED

bubble wrap,
  10 feet (3 m) long
duct tape
marker

MUSCLES USED

leg
arm
shoulder
back

TIME

10-15 minutes

1. Lay the bubble wrap flat on the floor. Tape the corners so it does not move.

2. Stand on one end of the bubble wrap. Your heels should be even with the edge.

3. Bend your knees. Swing your arms back and forth. Jump as far as you can. Listen for the pop when you land!

4. Make a mark where your heels landed on the bubble wrap.

5. Jump again. See if swinging your arms more helps you jump farther. Try bending your knees more and pushing off of your toes harder.

Jump-a-Roo

How high can you jump?

WHAT YOU NEED

yardstick
colored chalk
masking tape

MUSCLES USED

leg
arm
shoulder
back

TIME

5-10 minutes

1. Hold the **yardstick** against a wall. The zero end should reach the ground. Use **chalk** to mark the wall at the top of the yardstick. Ask for **permission** before drawing on the wall.

2. Move the yardstick up so the zero end is at the mark. Tape the yardstick to the wall.

3. Rub chalk on your fingers. Stand in front of the yardstick. Keep your back straight. Bend your knees.

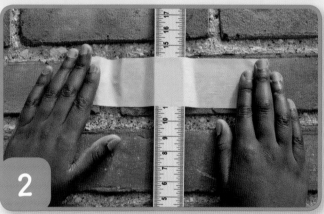

4. Jump up as high as you can and touch the yardstick. Land with your knees bent and feet flat on the ground.

5. Check your **fingerprints** to see how high you jumped. Jump four more times. What was your highest jump?

➡ Remember to clean the wall and yardstick when you are finished.

Zigzag

Jumping from side to side improves your balance!

WHAT YOU NEED

15-foot (4.5 m) rope

MUSCLES USED

leg
arm
shoulder
back
stomach

TIME

10-15 minutes

1. Lay the rope on the ground. Make it curve back and forth.

2. Stand at one end of the rope. The rope should be next to you. Keep your feet together. Bend your knees. Bend your elbows.

3. Jump **sideways** over the rope. **Switch** the position of your arms as you jump. Land with your feet together.

4. Jump back over the rope. Swing your arms the other way.

5. Keep jumping back and forth over the rope. Stop when you reach the end. Turn around and jump again. Try to go faster! Do it five times.

➡ Try it with another person. Criss-cross back and forth.

23

Shoe Jump

Jump over the swinging shoe!

WHAT YOU NEED

jump rope or any
   10-foot (3 m) rope
one athletic shoe

MUSCLES USED

leg

TIME

10-20 minutes

1. Tie one end of the rope to the shoe.

2. Have everyone stand in a circle. One person stands in the middle. He or she holds the end of the rope.

3. The person in the middle swings the rope in a circle along the ground.

4. The people in the circle jump over the shoe. See how many people can jump it before it hits someone's feet.

5. When it hits someone's feet, it is that person's turn to swing the rope.

➡ Try swinging the rope faster and slower and higher and lower. Make it harder for people to jump over the shoe every time.

Hopscotch

A game of balance everyone likes to play!

WHAT YOU NEED

chalk
small rock

MUSCLES USED

leg
arm
back

TIME

10-15 minutes

1. Ask for **permission** before drawing on the sidewalk with **chalk**. Draw squares to make the board. Number the squares 1 to 10.

2. Throw a rock into square 1. Hop over the rock to square 2. Keep hopping to the end of the board. Don't land with both feet in one square. If there are two squares next to each other, land with one foot in each square.

3. At the end, hop and turn in square 10. Then hop back. Stop in square 2 to pick up your rock. Then hop in square 1 and off the board.

4. Toss the rock into square 2. Hop up and down the board again. This time skip square 2.

5. On each turn, toss the rock into the next square. Remember to pick up your rock on the way back!

Circle Scotch

Challenge yourself to build better balance skills!

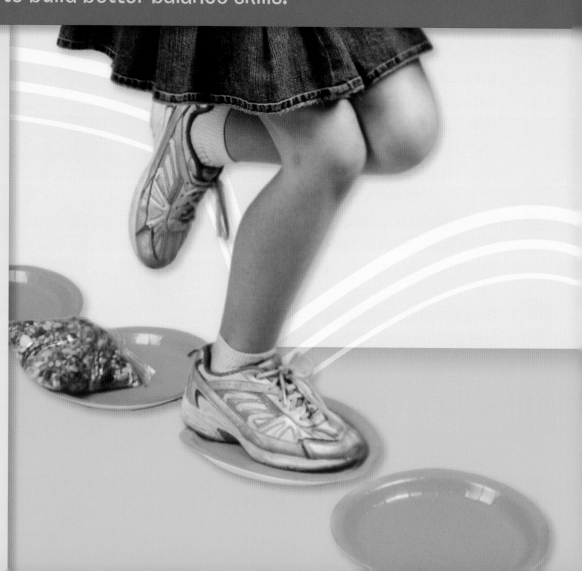

WHAT YOU NEED

large paper plates
masking tape
dried beans
zipper bag

MUSCLES USED

leg
back
stomach

TIME

10-15 minutes

1. Tape eight paper plates to the floor Leave space between each one.

2. Put some dried **beans** in a small zipper bag to make a bean bag. Throw the bean bag into the first circle.

3. Stand on one foot. Hop over the circle with the bean bag to the next circle. Keep hopping on one foot to the last circle. Turn around on one foot and hop back.

4. Don't land on both feet or outside the circles. If you do, start over with the bean bag in the same circle.

5. If you make it, throw the bean bag into the next circle. Keep going until you have tossed the bean bag into each circle.

Just Keep Moving!

Try these during TV and homework breaks, after meals, or anytime.

Trampoline Jump

Start jumping up and down. Swing your arms up and move your legs to each side at the same time.

One-Legged Foot Race

Hop on one foot to another room. Hop on the other foot back.

Squat Jumps

Squat down and put your hands on the floor. Now jump up as high as you can, swinging your arms up.

Hop Tag

Play this game with friends. Everyone hops or jumps to catch each other. No running allowed!

Pillowcase Hop

Step into a pillowcase. Hold the sides up and jump around the room.

Being active is for everyone!
- Ask your family to join in activities at home.
- Have relay races with your classmates at recess.
- Have an adult take you to a safe park to play tag with friends.

Super Simple Moves
Pledge

I promise to be active and move my body for one hour a day, five days a week.
I know that eating right and getting enough sleep are also important.
I want to be healthy and have a strong body.

I will:

☑ keep track of my activities on a Move It Chart or something like it

☑ ask my friends to stay active with me and set up play times outside three days a week

☑ ask my family to plan a physical activity one day a week

☑ limit my time watching TV and using the computer, except for homework

☑ get up and move my body during TV commercials and homework breaks

To print a pledge certificate, go to www.abdopublishing.com.
For more information about being active, please visit www.letsmove.gov.

31

Glossary

ankle – the part of your body where your foot meets your leg.

bean – a seed or a pod that you can eat. Also, something that looks like a bean but is not a bean, such as coffee beans and vanilla beans.

chalk – a stick made of soft rock used to write on blackboards and sidewalks.

chore – a regular job or task, such as cleaning your room.

column – one of the vertical rows in a table or chart.

energy – the ability to move, work, or play hard without getting tired.

fingerprint – the mark made by the ridges in the skin on a fingertip.

muscle – the tissue connected to the bones that allows body parts to move.

permission – when a person in charge says it's okay to do something.

serving – a single portion of food.

sideways – to or from the side.

switch – to change from one thing to another.

symbol – an object or picture that stands for or represents something.

yardstick – a measuring tool that is one yard long and marked in feet and inches.